Clam Digging & Crabbing
in
California

an informative guide on
clam digging and crabbing
in California.

by
John A. Johnson
and
Jon C. Weber

Table of Contents

Clamming & Crabbing
in
California

©Copyright 1993
John A. Johnson
and
Jon C. Weber

ISBN 0-937861-17-0

FIRST PRINTING, JANUARY 1993

ADVENTURE NORTH PUBLISHING CO.
P.O. Box 1601 • Waldport, Oregon 97394
Printed in the USA
Wegferd Publications
North Bend, Oregon 97459

Jon C. Weber & John A. Johnson

Acknowledgements

I wish to thank my stepfather, Gordon Walker, who taught me about living in the great Northwest and how to enjoy its many wonders.

I'd also like to thank my best friend John Johnson with whom I am co-writing this book. We've been friends since the sixth grade and have participated in many adventures reminiscent of *Indiana Jones and the Lost Temple*. I am looking forward to having many more.

Thanks also to my other best friend, Lieutenant Jayne E. Campbell (U.S. Navy), my outdoor partner who is teaching me a new way of enjoying the great outdoors by sharing it with those who haven't known it and loved it like I do.

I also want to thank Bob Tasto, Jim Hardwick, John Sunada, Bob Hardy and all of the dedicated biologists with the California Department of Fish and Game. Many of the excellent maps, tables and information contained in this guide were provided by their efforts. Without their advice and assistance, this book could not have been produced.

And also a special thanks to Mari (Palmer) Van Dyke. Her maps and realistic drawings added a special touch to this book.

Jon C. Weber

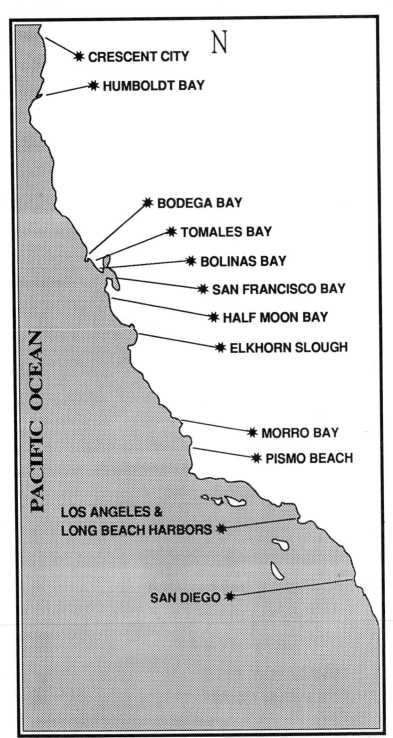

N

★ CRESCENT CITY

★ HUMBOLDT BAY

★ BODEGA BAY

★ TOMALES BAY

★ BOLINAS BAY

★ SAN FRANCISCO BAY

★ HALF MOON BAY

★ ELKHORN SLOUGH

PACIFIC OCEAN

★ MORRO BAY

★ PISMO BEACH

LOS ANGELES &
LONG BEACH HARBORS ★

SAN DIEGO ★

Courtesy California Department of Fish & Game

8

INTRODUCTION

My fondest memories are of my school days growing up in Seaside, Oregon on the Northwest Oregon Coast. It was a great time to be a kid, and the northwest coast of Oregon was the greatest place on earth to learn the many simple lessons of life. That time still had an innocence with few of the problems kids face nowadays. It was also a paradise — truly a land of plenty where my best friends and I enjoyed unending adventures while hunting, fishing, exploring and enjoying some of the finest clamming and crabbing anywhere south of Alaska.

In the latter part of 1967 I joined the Army and moved away from my home in Oregon searching for a new kind of adventure in a different part of the world. I am still involved in this great adventure as I write this book, and although I have never really regretted leaving my home, family and friends in Oregon and Washington, I could never forget them either. During my many return visits it is rare not to find me on a beach or river during a low tide in hot pursuit of clams or crabs. These precious hours are the most pleasant, relaxing, and renewing experiences I have ever known.

I've traveled to many parts of the world. I am always drawn to the beaches, bays and riverfronts to see if it might not bring me somehow closer to "home" as I looked for clamming and crabbing opportunities. Sadly, I have never found anything to compare with the shellfish resources available to those fortunate enough to reside on the west coast of the United States. It is truly a horn of plenty for anyone willing to put forth a little research, elbow grease, and a desire for some fun, fresh air and a little adventure.

I have been stationed in California twice in my 25 years with the Army and could never find any general reference book on clam digging or crabbing in California — and so this book.

It is my hope, that by writing this book on clam digging and crabbing in California, to open the eyes of some California residents and seasonal travelers to the truly unique outdoor opportunity available on their beaches. In addition to good family oriented outdoor fun, this book will guide the seafood gourmet to unlimited seafood delights.

In a few short months from now I will conclude my great adventure with the United States Army, and I will be returning to my home on the Oregon Coast where I was born, raised and hopefully will spend the rest of my days. You can bet that a good portion of that time will be spent on as many of the beaches, bays and rivers in the Northwest as the good Lord will allow. I will be enjoying what has made me the happiest: being close to nature with my friends, digging up a mess of clams, and cooking up a pot of fresh Dungeness crabs. For me, as the popular TV ad says, "It doesn't get much better than that."

In your pursuit of clams and crabs, please remember that these resources are not inexhaustible but are a delicate part of our fragile ecosystem. Please take only what you need. Obey all regulations, don't litter, and try to adopt an attitude of conservation for our bounty. We will all have to do our part if we are to preserve what we have so that future generations can enjoy California's gift to all.

Jon C. Weber

Shells from the species of clams most commonly dug in California estuaries.
1. Gaper 2. Washington 3. Cockle 4. Littlenecks 5. Pismo
6. Mussel 7. Geoduck 8. Softshell 9. Chione 10. Razor

CLAM DIGGING IN CALIFORNIA

Residents and visitors to western California who enjoy good clam digging are fortunate indeed. Few states can match the quantity, quality and variety of clam species available. Just imagine, 43 species of clams and eight species of mussels reside in California's coastal waters. Great scenery, fresh salt air and super outdoor exercise await those who pursue these shellfish. No matter what your wish might be, from tiny littleneck clams to 8-pound geoducks, or fast digging razor clams, California can be a clam digger's paradise.

We have written this book concentrating on those clam species that are common enough and in sufficient quantity to adequately support a clam fishery and reward the average clam digger for an honest effort. We have therefore limited the species covered to nine clams and two mussels.

The management of this valuable resource is in the hands of dedicated biologists working for the California Department of Fish and Game. Without their scientific study, protection and enhancement efforts, the fragile clam population on the California Coast could easily be just a memory of the way it was in "the good old days." Whether replacing lost habitat, purchasing more public access sites, or rebuilding a clam population after a natural decline, the dedication of California's biologists is to be applauded.

Anyone digging clams in the state of California must possess a fishing license as per state regulations. These fees help fund projects that will enhance the future populations of clams in the state so that our children might enjoy this same resource.

Stan and Margaret Johnson

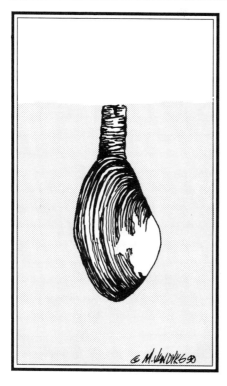

e. M. VanDyke 90

GAPER
CLAM
(Tresus capax)

The gaper clam has a variety of common names depending on where you are on the West Coast. Around Coos Bay, Oregon it is called the empire clam, and in Tillamook, Oregon it is known as the blue or blue neck, because of the blue color of the meat near the tip of the neck. In the state of Washington it is most often called the horse clam because of its large neck. In parts of California it is called the horse neck clam, but it is most often called the gaper clam because of the opening or "gape" near the posterior end of the shell.

Whatever you call it, the gaper clam is quite large, second only to the enormous geoduck clam. A mature clam will have a shell up to 8 inches in length and weigh up to 5 pounds. The total weight of the dressed clammeat ranges from 15 to 35 percent of its total weight depending on the season. One big gaper clam fried whole will feed an average person nicely, but be sure to pound the tough neck before cooking or get ready for cramps in your jaw muscles.

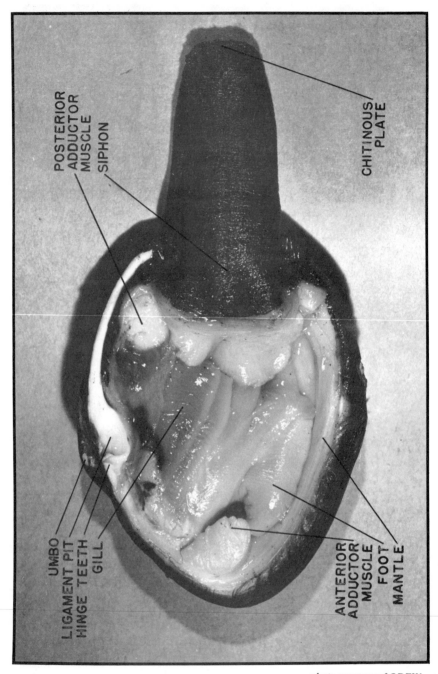

POSTERIOR ADDUCTOR MUSCLE

SIPHON

CHITINOUS PLATE

UMBO

LIGAMENT PIT

HINGE TEETH

GILL

ANTERIOR ADDUCTOR MUSCLE

FOOT

MANTLE

photo courtesy of ODFW

This is a Gaper clam, however, other clams look basically the same when the shell is removed.

Gaper clams can get quite large. This clam weighs nearly three pounds. A few of these and you've got a meal.

Gapers live in a mud-sand substrate type in bays, sloughs and estuaries as well as more quiet sheltered areas along the outer coast. They are rather evenly distributed throughout the state. It is probably one of the most common clams along the entire coast of California and it ranges from near the high tide line into water over 100 feet deep. The best localities include Alamitos, Morro, Tomales, Bodega and Humboldt bays, and Elkhorn Slough. It is highly esteemed for food and is the object of a heavy sportfishery, especially in Central and Northern California.

The presence of gaper clams is revealed by looking for their siphons or a disturbance of the surface while you are walking or pounding. Gapers are found from 12 to 30 inches beneath the surface of the mudflat. They extend the tip of their necks to the surface to feed. Unlike razor clams, the gaper does not dig down after being disturbed, but remains stationary. When disturbed, the huge neck is pulled down revealing a large hole 1 inch or greater in size. It may occasionally be located when the siphons are withdrawn rapidly enough to squirt water several feet into the air. The top of its neck can often be seen but is usually camouflaged with its brown skin flaps or thickly attached algae. The suction felt by probing a suspected clam hole with your finger is a dead give away that you have found a gaper clam or possibly a geoduck.

Now the work begins. Much physical effort is required to capture this clam. A good shovel with a wide blade is a necessity. Dig rapidly just to the side of the siphon to prevent breakage and to prevent the mud or sand from caving in. When you reach the clam, it is often awkward to bring it to the surface because it is difficult to grip. A secret I've learned is to stick my thumb in the "gape" next to the neck and pull slowly with the thumb and forefinger. Don't try to retrieve the clam by gripping the neck — it will inevitably break and you will lose the clam, and it will die.

A proven method used by knowledgeable diggers is to cut out the bottom of a 5-gallon bucket, placing it down over the clam hole as you dig. Work it down as you dig and this will prevent collapsing of the clam hole, allowing you to retrieve the clam with much less effort. Large holes often remain after digging gaper clams. Be sure to fill them in. It helps improve habitat and eliminates a safety hazard.

Gaper clam diggers usually need a good minus time for best results.

Jason Campbell with an average-sized Gaper clam.

PREPARATION FOR THE TABLE

CLEANING —

To clean a gaper clam, the procedure is very similar to cleaning a razor clam with one exception. A thick, leathery skin covers the large neck of a gaper and can be very difficult to remove. Separate the neck and the foot. Soak the neck in near-boiling water for about 3 minutes or freeze the necks overnight and the tough skin can then be easily removed.

COOKING —

Gaper clams have a flavor second only to the razor clam in my opinion. They can be fried in batter, made into fritters, or they make excellent chowder. The neck of a gaper clam is as tough as leather and must be tenderized by thorough pounding. A single fried neck from one of these huge clams will nearly fill an average dinner plate.

Dan Campbell uses a section of metal pipe to help him reach a deep Gaper clam.

Herb Hoppe with a good Gaper Clam.

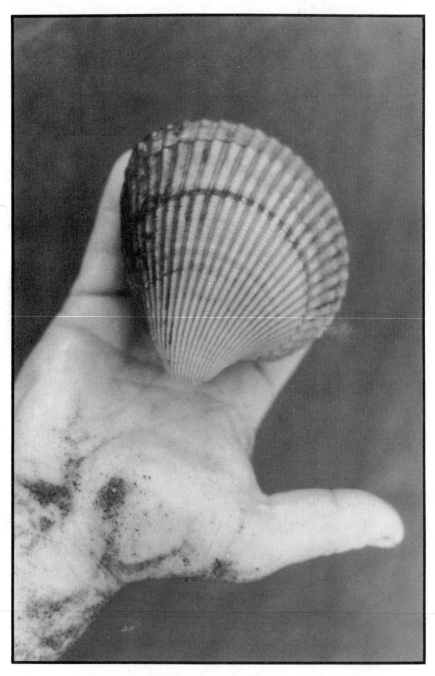

Cockles are a fairly large clam and make excellent clam chowder or fritters.

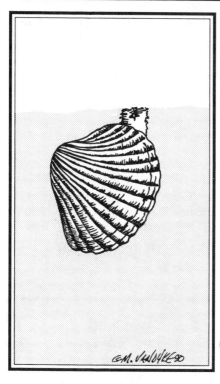

G.M. VAN DYKE 90

COCKLE
CLAM
(Clinocardium nuttalli)

The cockle is a 2 to 4-inch clam that can be easily identified by its many prominent and evenly spaced ridges on the exterior of the shell. Other names for the cockle are basket cockle and quahog. Its color will vary from a light brown when found in sand to a darker gray when the habitat is muddy.

Cockles are found in many bays along the California Coast and are popular clams in terms of recreational harvest. They can be found in the mud and sandy mudflats of the lower bay areas. They are most common in Humboldt, Bolinas, Half Moon bays, and Elkhorn Slough.

The cockle has a very short neck and therefore is found near the surface from 1 to 3 inches deep. The "show" is difficult to detect, sometimes showing up as a small double hole less than 1/2 inch total length.

A rake is the best and most common way to gather cockles. The standard garden variety with 3-inch tines does a great job. Should the holes be readily visible, as they are on rare occasions, a shovel works well for digging individual clams.

Cockles are most often eaten as steamers or in clam chowder. Some folks will also fry them whole. In any case, leave the clams overnight in clean salt water and allow them to pump themselves free of sand. Cleaning is accomplished by steaming or dropping the clams directly into boiling water until the shells pop open (it only takes a few short seconds). Further cleaning of the clam is unnecessary. Dip these clams into melted butter and lemon juice and the taste is pure heaven.

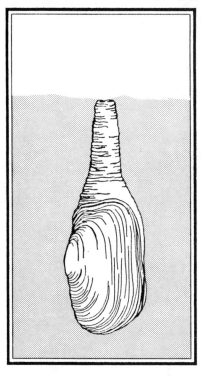

GEODUCK
CLAM
(Panope generosa)

The geoduck (pronounced *goo'-ee-duck*) is the world's largest burrowing clam, reaching a weight of 10 pounds. A 5-pound geoduck with a stretched out length of 3 feet is not at all uncommon!

The state of California has a limited population of geoduck clams. Beds are known to exist in Humboldt, Tomales, Bolinas and Morro bays. The bad news is that most of these clams are subtidal, meaning they live below the low tide level, and cannot be reached by the sport digger. Commercial fisheries in the Northwest harvest these giants with hard hat divers at great depths.

Geoducks are considered real trophies to sport clam diggers for several reasons. They are relatively rare and hard to find, and even then they are only harvested at very low tides. They are difficult to dig since they live buried in the mud 2 to 4 feet deep or better. Finally, their large size and succulent flavor make these clams a real prize.

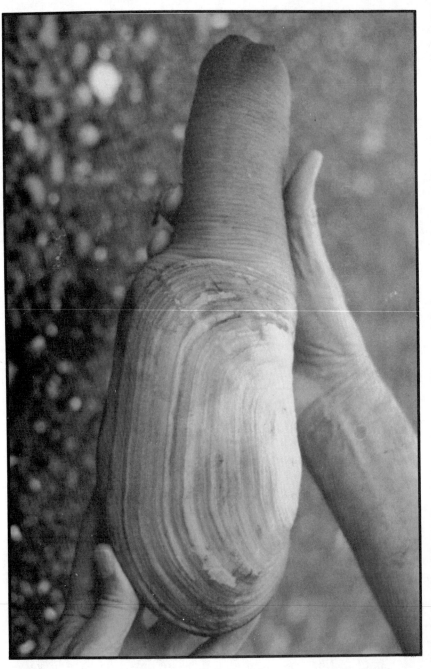

The largest of all California clams, the Geoduck clam can weigh up to ten pounds.

HOW TO DIG

The body and shell of geoducks are buried quite deep, but they must extend their long necks to the surface to feed. Their large siphon will remain at surface level until they are disturbed by a person's poke with a finger, pounding with a shovel handle or stomping with the feet. When disturbed, they withdraw their neck downward, creating an easily identifiable 1 to 2-inch hole. At very low tides these clams can sometimes be located on mudflats by streams of water which the clam may squirt several feet into the air.

Now the effort begins. Start digging slightly off to one side to prevent crushing this thin-shelled clam. Use a large open-holed cylinder made from a bottomless 5-gallon plastic bucket to prevent the sides of the hole from falling in. When you reach the clam neck, do not attempt to pull the clam up by its neck; it will usually pull off. You must dig deeper to free the body portion.

Capturing a Geoduck is hard work and messy business. Be prepared to dig deep.

photo courtesy of Washington Department of Fisheries.

Geoducks can extend their necks a long way to feed near the surface.

Typical gear for Geoduck harvest. The metal pipes prevent the hole from caving in and allow the digger to go deep where they live.

PREPARATION FOR THE TABLE

CLEANING —

A geoduck is a huge clam, but is cleaned like its smaller cousins. Cut the four adductor muscles and free the meat from the shell. Separate the neck and remove the thick outer skin by dropping it into boiling water for a few seconds. Cut off the tip of the siphon, and slit the neck from top to bottom. Cut away the gills and clean out all the dark intestines from the "boot" of the clam. Cut the neck into smaller pieces and pound thoroughly if you intend to fry them. Also, the entire clam can be ground for fritters or chowder.

COOKING —

Geoduck clammeat has a superb and unique flavor. Fried whole, in chowder or as fritters, this is some of California's finest seafood. Never overcook this delicacy!

Al Scholz, Shellfish Biologist with the Washington Department of Fisheries with an average-sized Geoduck weighing about five pounds.

Littlenecks or Steamer clams are small but superb tablefare when steamed and dipped in melted butter and lemon juice.

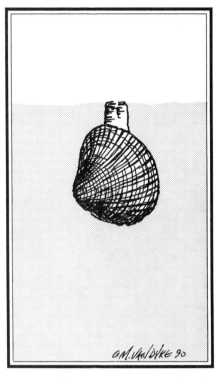

LITTLENECK
CLAM

(Prototaca staminea
and
Tapes japanica)

The littleneck clam is quite small and averages only about 2 to 3 inches in size. Also called steamer, butter, rock cockle and Japanese cockle, it is similar in appearance to the cockle in that the radiating ribs are visible, but they are much less prominent than those of the cockle. Two species of littlenecks, which are quite similar in appearance, inhabit California waters: the Manila and the common. Littlenecks are the most commonly harvested clam, by number, in California.

The littleneck is well distributed throughout the coastline of California. They are found in coarse sand and gravel areas near the low tide line. It is found from 1 to 3 inches beneath the surface and is often picked up incidentally while raking for cockles or other shallow dwelling clams. Their hole is shaped like a keyhole and is 1/4 to 1/2 inch long. In areas of heavy concentration, they can be dug by turning over the sand and gravel with a rake, pitchfork or shovel, but a rake with 3 to 6-inch dull tines is the preferred tool.

Littlenecks are the clams you get when you order steamers in restaurants, and they are most often prepared that way. They make superb tablefare when dipped in a mixture of butter and lemon juice, after steaming them open. Like cockles, they should be left overnight in clean salt water so they will pump themselves free of sand.

Raking for Steamers.

Littleneck clams are normally found in a gravel/sand substrate. A long-tined rake is the best way to gather steamers.

A long-tined rake such as this one works great in gravel.

The Pismo clam is fairly large and hard shelled.

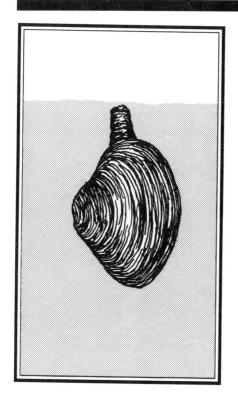

PISMO
CLAM
(Tivela sultorum)

The Pismo clam is a relatively large bivalve. It can attain a length of 6 inches although specimens up to 7 inches have been dug. The meat of the Pismo is highly esteemed, and it is the subject of an extremely heavy sport fishery in California.

Pismo clams can be found in the intertidal zone on flat, sandy beaches of the open coast fully exposed to the full force of the surf. They are usually found within 6 inches of the surface. Their range is from Morro Bay to Mexico. They are sometimes found in the entrance channels to bays, sloughs or estuaries. The best localities for sport harvesting are at Pismo Beach, Grover City, Oceano, Morro Bay, and the area in Monterey Bay between Elkhorn Slough and Santa Cruz. They are, however, common along many of the sandy beaches in California.

Common equipment for Pismo clam harvest, a fork with handy measuring device.

Probably the most common method of taking the Pismo clam is with a 6-tine pitchfork or a potato fork. The digger works backward in a line parallel to the edge of the water, probing until striking a clam. The clam is then lifted out, measured and, if legal, may be taken. *(See "Regulations Section" on page 60 for legal sizes.)* A commercially available or homemade measuring device is attached to the handle to make this task quick and simple. This method enhances the probability of locating the clam and also allows the digger to watch out for the heavy waves that occasionally strike.

During some times of the year and on some beaches, clams can be located on the exposed flats and sand bars by looking for either holes or mounds of sand at the surface. Both holes and sand mounds are made by water forced out through the siphons when the clam digs deeper.

Many undersized clams are dug up in the course of harvesting. The mortality on these undersized clams can be devastating if they are not immediately reburied. Seagulls by the hundreds scavenge the beaches looking for clams left high and dry by thoughtless diggers. The birds, with clam in mouth, fly to great heights and drop the clams onto the hard-packed sand which causes the shell to break. California law and common sense require that all undersized clams be immediately reburied in the sand. This simple act will insure the future of Pismo clams. We must do everything we can to protect this valuable resource. Perhaps the easiest method to comply with this law is to dig out a forkful of sand, place the undersized clam in the resulting hole and then "replace the divot." Clams buried in this manner should be so placed that the dark knobby hinge ligament is up.

The areas near Grover City and Oceano are open to wheeled vehicle travel so be safe and be careful!

Everyone in the family can enjoy clamming at Pismo Beach.

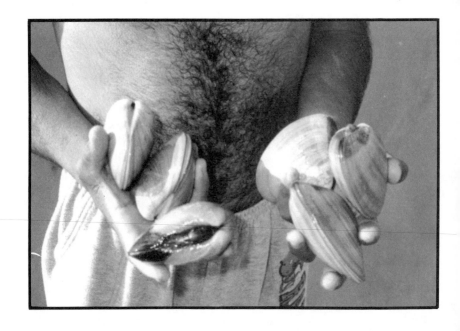

PREPARATION FOR THE TABLE

CLEANING —

Clams left undisturbed for a short time will open their shells slightly. A knife can then be inserted in the opening and the adductor muscles severed. Another method is to freeze the clam until the muscles relax. Sever the remaining adductor muscles close to the shell. Once the clam is opened and removed from the shell, the meat is ready for trimming.

Remove the siphons, mantle and gills. The four adductor muscles should be trimmed next. Then, remove the dark thumbnail-sized liver and discard it. Trim the hard edge of the digging foot and you'll have a section of soft tissue about the diameter of a silver dollar. Cut through it lengthwise then remove and discard the intestine. This is easily done with the fingers. You'll then have three piles of meat, one with the four adductor muscles, another with the two dollar-sized pieces of the foot and one with the trimmed off pieces (mantle, siphons, etc.).

COOKING —

Pismo clams have an excellent flavor and can be fried, ground up into chowder, and the adductor "buttons" can be used raw as a seafood cocktail. However you prepare them, you will have a gourmet's delight.

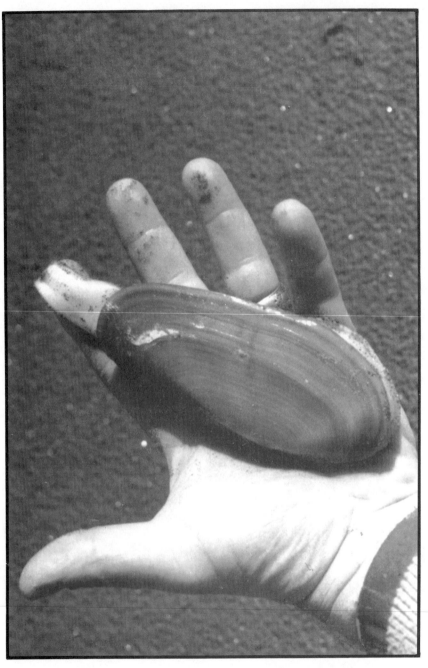

Many people believe the Razor clam is the best eating of all California clams.

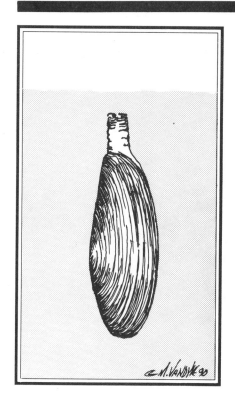

RAZOR
CLAM
(Siliqua patula)

The razor clam is the shining jewel along Northern California's wind swept beaches and bleached white sand. It is one of the most highly prized clams. The reasons for this are as varied as the sport diggers I have interviewed. Most agree that the razor clam is the best eating of all bivalves on the West Coast. They are usually dug along the picturesque beaches of Northern California in clean sand that is free of rocks and debris and is pounded by the rolling surf. Many will tell you that digging razor clams is truly a sporting experience and a real challenge. They are the only California clam species that, upon being disturbed, will rapidly dig deeper to avoid capture. Another reason may be that a razor clam is relatively easy to clean and yields a high percentage of edible meat. No matter what the reason, the razor clam is truly supreme among California's clam species and unquestionably my own personal favorite.

Digging Razor clams in the "surf" is challenging and pure fun!

Kai Johnson with a nice mess of clams.

Stan Johnson

The razor clam's scientific name, *Siliqua patula,* literally means "spreading foot," which refers to the muscular foot or digger. Razors actually dig by combining water with muscle action to spread this "foot" and pull the body downward into the sand. The thin oval-shaped shell, covered with a smooth brown glossy covering, reduces resistance. These features, combined with a powerful digger, allows the clam to rapidly pull itself downward. A razor clam can dig up to 9 inches a minute in soft sand. Vertical movement is common, but horizontal movement of an adult clam from one location to another has never been observed.

Razor clams spawn in late spring or early summer at 2 years of age or older. Eggs and sperm are broadcast in the ocean when water temperatures reach 55 degrees F. Young clams grow fast and reach 1 inch in a few weeks and 3 to 4 inches in one year. Razors can live to be 4 to 5 years of age and measure 5 inches in length. An 8 year old clam is considered a real grandpa!

Low tide allows the digger to approach the clam where he lives. *How low* is the question. A minus tide is considered best because the lower margins of the beach are where the greatest concentrations of clams are found. Generally speaking, a 1-foot minus tide or better provides the best digging opportunity. I have, however, dug limits of razors on a +.5-foot low tide when ocean conditions were very calm.

Calm ocean conditions are an important consideration when digging razor clams. Rough surf retards feeding activity and also makes it difficult to see the bottom when digging in the water. A rough ocean can also be a real safety hazard. More than one razor clam digger has lost his life during such conditions. A good rule of thumb is to dig 90 minutes before a low tide until one hour after low tide. Tide books can be purchased at most sport shops and hardware stores along the coast.

A stainless steel shovel is expensive but well worth the extra cost.

John Johnson and his mother.

TOOLS AND EQUIPMENT

Any narrow-bladed shovel which allows the digger to extract a wedge of sand from the surface will do. I prefer a straight blade, 5 inches wide by 8 inches long with a slight "cup" to it. Custom clam shovels made of stainless steel are available, but they are expensive!

Some diggers prefer using a "clam gun" which is a metal tube 2 feet long and 5 inches in diameter. It has a handle and is open at one end. It is inserted over the clam hole and when extracted, a column of sand is removed, and hopefully, so is the clam.

Any porous container can be used to carry your catch. If you can attach it to your belt, all the better. A small burlap or nylon mesh sack is great.

Good hip boots are a must and chest waders are even better. A wet clam digger is an unhappy clam digger.

HOW TO DIG

There are basically two methods of digging razors: in the water and in the "dry" sand. Most beginners will dig in the "dry" (actually quite wet) sand as it is easy to find the "show" or dimple left after a disturbed clam pulls its neck in and begins to dig down. The depression is usually 1/4 to 1/2-inch in size. Stomping on the sand with your feet or shovel handle will usually cause a clam to "show." A razor clam will be found anywhere from 6 inches to 3 feet beneath the surface. They always dig down at an angle toward the ocean. A clammer must dig on the ocean side of the show to intercept the clam as it digs to escape. Only experience will tell you just how far away from the "show" to dig, but a good rule of thumb is about 6 inches. Most experienced razor clammers prefer digging in the water.

Wade out into a foot or so of water and, when the water is clear enough to see the bottom, pound with your shovel handle. A disturbed clam will show a puff of sand or a depression about 1/2 inch in diameter as it pulls its neck down and begins to dig away. Experiences and speed are the ingredients for successful razor digging. You'll feel a real sense of accomplishment when you sack your first limit of razors while digging in the surf.

PREPARATION FOR THE TABLE

CLEANING —

Cleaning a razor clam is relatively simple. First, separate the animal and shell. A short, sharp, thin-bladed knife can be used to slide down each side of the shell cutting the round adductor muscles. The whole clam can then be easily removed from the shell.

A much easier and less messy procedure is to simply drop the clams into boiling water for a few short seconds until the shells pop open. Now, immediately place the clams into cold water so as not to overcook them. The meat and shell will easily separate. It should be emphasized that boiling the clams too long will overcook the meat and ruin the flavor and texture.

Now you are ready to clean the clam. With a knife, separate the neck (or siphon) and the foot. Cut the brown tip off the neck and split it lengthwise. Split the foot lengthwise and scrape out all dark colored organs. Wash the meat thoroughly and it is ready to be cooked.

COOKING —

Razors may be battered and fried whole, ground up and cooked as fritters, or made into clam chowder. The best way to ruin a good batch of fried clams is to overcook them. Cook on each side for 30 seconds at 350 degrees in a well-greased pan and better seafood you won't find anywhere.

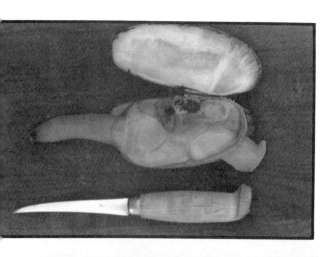

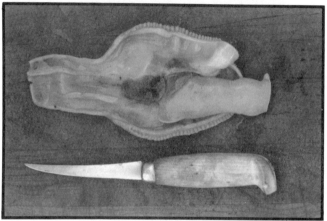

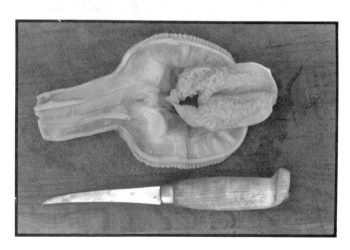

How a Razor clam is cleaned. Other clams can be cleaned in a similar manner once they are out of the shell.

A good mess of Softshells is well worth the effort. They make excellent chowder and are great fried.

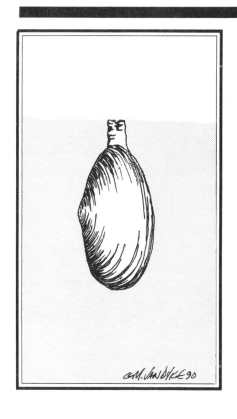

SOFTSHELL
CLAM
(Mya arenaria)

The softshell clam is a native of the eastern seaboard and was accidentally introduced to the West Coast in the late 1800s. This clam is commonly called the eastern softshell, steamer or mud clam. The softshell is one of California's most overlooked and underutilized major clam species.

It is a medium-sized clam, ranging from 4 to 6 inches in length and 1/4 to 1/2 pound in weight at maturity. This oval-shaped clam usually has a chalky-white, brittle shell that is extremely sharp. Cut fingers are a common occurrence among diggers and many will wear rubber gloves to prevent this problem.

Like the gaper clam, softshell clams have a very long neck that allows them to live 6 to 20 inches beneath the surface. It extends the tip of its neck to the surface to feed, extracting food organisms from the water. The softshell is also similar to the gaper in that it can retract its long neck, but the body remains stationary and invisible deep in the mud. These clams prefer a muddy substrate, although it is not really uncommon to find softshells in the sand. Some softshells live below the tide line (subtidal), but most are intertidal. A minus tide is not necessary to reach them. Any reasonably low tide is usually sufficient to expose their beds.

The best localities for harvesting this clam are Tomales, Bodega and Humboldt bays, and Elkhorn Slough. You'll find them in back areas near the influx of fresh water.

A good Softshell will weight a half pound and is great eating.

HOW TO DIG

The softshell's siphon hole or "show" is detected by an oblong hole up to 3/4 inch long that is sometimes hard to see in soft mud, but once recognized the clam is easily located. You can often feel the neck retract by sticking your finger into the hole. Ghost shrimp (sand shrimp) and softshells frequently live in the same area and surface holes look similar. Beneath the surface, ghost shrimp create a maze of tunnels going all directions, whereas a clam hole is always vertical.

Any good garden shovel will do for digging softshells. There are basically two ways to dig them. Either dig individual holes or find a good concentration of clams and simply dig a trench about 2-feet deep and pluck the clams as they are exposed. Be sure to fill in your holes and trenches.

To dig these clams individually, start digging slightly off to one side so as not to crush the clam with the shovel. When you find the clam (6 to 20 inches down), gently grasp the whole shell and pull it out, being careful not to cut your fingers. Don't try to pull up a softshell by the neck as it will usually break off.

Softshell digging is a messy sport at best. It is smart to wear a pair of waders and rain gear top and bottom. These bivalves are not called "mud clams" for nothing!

Extremely low tides are not necessary for good Softshell digging

Dig one large hole when Softshells are numerous.

Getting wet is part of the fun of clamming.

PREPARATION FOR THE TABLE

CLEANING —

Small softshells make excellent steamer clams and can be eaten whole when so prepared. In fact, softshells are commonly called steamers on the East Coast because that is how they are most often eaten. Be sure to soak the clams for at least 12 hours in clean, cool salt water so that they will pump their systems clean.

Large softshells are best cleaned by first soaking them in near boiling water for about 3 minutes. This pops the shell open and allows the clam to be pulled free or easily cut from the shell. It also makes easy the removal of the clear slimy coating that covers the neck. Then, follow the same procedure used to clean razor and gaper clams.

COOKING —

Eastern softshells have excellent flavor quite similar to that of razors. They can be fried whole, ground up for fritters, or used in clam chowder.

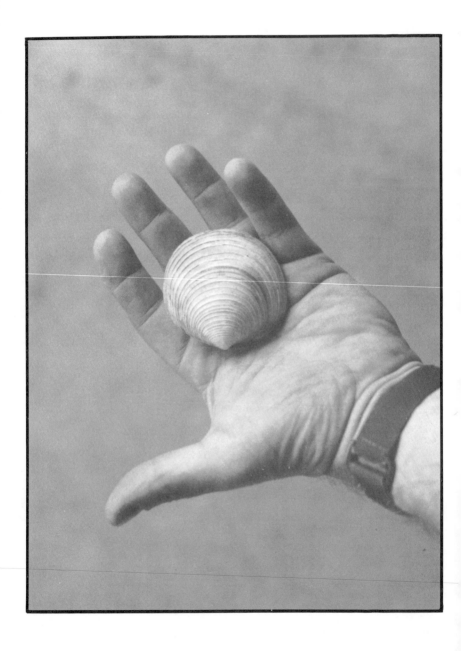

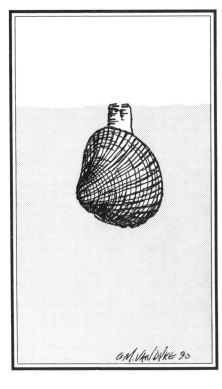

G.M.VANDYKE 90

CHIONE CLAM

(Chione fluctifraga, undatella and californienses)

The chione (pronounced *kee-oon'-ee*) is a medium-sized clam reaching lengths of 2-1/2 to 3-1/2 inches in size. Also called bay, mud or hard-shelled cockle, its range is limited to Southern California's bays, sloughs and estuaries. These clams provide one of the more popular sport and commercial fisheries in the southern part of the state. Best locations to find chiones include Alamitos, Newport and San Diego bays, and Anaheim and Tijuana sloughs.

Three species of chiones are found in Southern California. They are the *smooth, wavy* and *banded*. Chiones are found in the mudflats or back bays and sloughs. They live at or very near the surface and, once located, are dug with rakes or small hand spades.

These clams are highly prized for their flavor and are prepared in much the same way as steamers.

A fairly large clam, the Butter clam has a thick heavy shell and very tasty meat.

A clam digger after Butter clams.

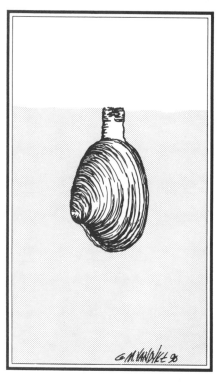

G.M. VANDYKE 90

WASHINGTON CLAM

*(Saxidomus nuttalli
and
Saxidomus giganteus)*

The Washington clam is also called the butter clam, quahog and sea cockle. It is identified by its 2 to 4-inch heavy ovate shell that shows fine concentric lines of growth on the exterior. A large Washington clam will reach 6 inches in length and weigh nearly 1 pound.

Washington's are one of the more important clams in the sheltered waters north of Morro Bay. The best localities in California are Morro, Bodega, Tomales and Humboldt bays, and Elkhorn Slough. These clams usually inhabit a gravel/sand mixture from a +1 foot tide level to the subtidal area. They are found 6 to 18 inches beneath the surface and a long-tined rake, shovel, or potato fork can be used to dig this species. The hole or "show" of this clam is cigar or keyhole shaped and is 1/2 to 3/4 inch long.

The meat of a Washington clam has an excellent flavor and texture. They can be fried, used for chowder, or eaten as steamers.

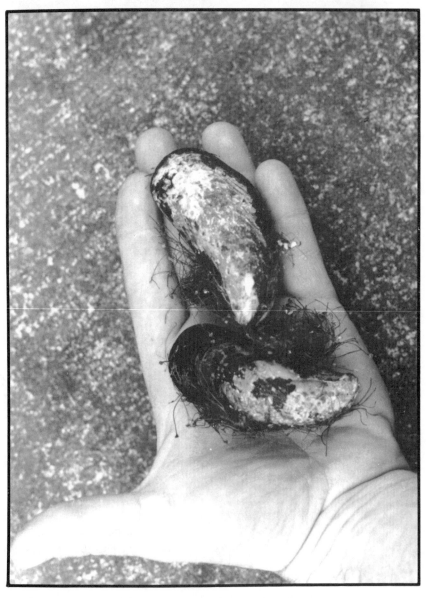

Mussels that are three to five inches long are the best eating size.

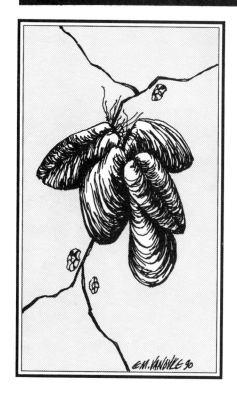

MUSSELS

Mussels are bivalve mollusks that inhabit the intertidal and subtidal areas along the California Coast. They live in clusters connected to rocks or other solid objects, by byssal threads which are secreted to form solid hold-downs. These byssal threads are often called the "beard" of the mussel.

Mussels, like oysters and clams, have long been one of modern and ancient man's favorite seafoods, especially here in California. The importance of mussels to the diet of coastal Indians can easily be observed by examining the remains of clam middens, or shell piles, found along the California coastline. In many locations they appear to represent the bulk of food items consumed by prehistoric man along the entire West Coast. When the tide was out, their table was set.

Mussels are still enjoyed around the world and are probably most famous in France where they are a prized delicacy. They are in such demand in Europe that thousands of tons of these black-shelled mollusks are raised each year through the practice of aquaculture farming. Sea ranches are successfully culturing native mussels to fill the growing demand of gourmet restaurants.

Two species of mussels commonly grow in California waters. The blue, or bay mussel, (*Mytilus Edulis*) is common to bays and sheltered areas. It has a smooth, blue-black or olive color to the shell and reaches a maximum length of about 3 inches.

The surf mussel, or California mussel, (*Mytilus Californianus*) is found along the rocky coastline, in large beds and may reach a length of 10 inches. Wherever you find rock outcroppings, you will likely find surf mussels.

The best time to sport harvest mussels is during winter months when peak yields of meat occur. Users will find 2 to 4-inch mussels collected from the lowest tide make the best eating. Be aware that Pacific Ocean mussels should be avoided during the months of June to September and chiefly in July and August. During this period, fatal cases of highly toxic paralytic shellfish poisoning (PSP) occur. It is best to contact the California Department of Fish and Wildlife prior to harvesting mussels. The Department follows the condition of all bivalves carefully throughout the year and, they have established a quarantine on mussels between May 1 and October 30.

Gathering mussels is probably the easiest of all seafood quests. You find the mussels, put your hands on one, and give several twists to break the "beard" free of its attachment. A 3-prong garden rake is also helpful in this task. Gloves are definitely a good idea or the sharp shells can easily cut your fingers. Now wash off the mussels and they are ready to steam open.

Any way you prepare a clam to eat, you can do the same with mussels. These edible mollusks, eaten as steamers and dipped in seafood sauce, are great. I have also enjoyed mussels deep fried in a thick batter.

Mussel gathering is fun and quite easy.

REGULATIONS

CLAMS, HARDSHELL and SOFTSHELL

- See California Sport Fishing Regulations for additional information on equipment, current limits and closures.
- Size is measured in greatest shell diameter.
- Fishing hours are one-half hour before sunrise to one-half hour after sunset.
- Spades, shovels, hoes, rakes or other appliances operated by hand, except spears or gaff hooks, may be used to take clams.
- Only authorized persons cleaning, repairing or maintaining beaches may possess such tools during non-fishing hours.
- Persons digging clams must possess a valid fishing license per state fishing regulations.

Species	Area	Season	Size Limit	Daily Limit
Gaper and Washington Clams	Humboldt Bay	Entire year	Note 1	50; only 25 may be gapers
Geoduck	Entire state	Entire year	Note 1	3
Littleneck, soft-shell, Chiones, Northern Quahog and Cockles	Entire state	Entire year	1-1/2 inch except no size limit on softshell. All softshell taken must be counted.	50 in combination
Pismo Clam	Santa Cruz and Monterey Counties	Sep 1 - Apr 30	Note 2	10
	Remainder of state	Entire year	Note 2	10
	Marine life refuges and clam preserves	Closed	Closed	Closed

Species	Area	Season	Size Limit	Daily Limit
Razor Clam	Between Mad River and Strawberry Creek (Humboldt County)	Entire even-numbered years	Note 1	First 20 dug
	Between Strawberry Creek and Moonstone Beach (Humboldt County)	Entire odd-numbered years	Note 1	First 20 dug
	North of Battery Pt (Del Norte County)	Entire odd-numbered years	Note 1	First 20 dug
	South of Battery Pt (Del Norte County)	Entire even-numbered years	Note 1	First 20 dug
	Remainder of state	Entire year	Note 1	First 20 dug
Mussels (Sea and Bay)	Entire state	Entire year	None	10 pounds (in the shell)

1) All clams dug, regardless of size or broken condition, must be retained as part of the daily limit.
2) 5 inches in greatest size diameter north of the boundary between San Luis Obispo and Monterey counties; 4-1/2 inches in greatest shell diameter south of the boundary between San Luis Obispo and Monterey counties.

RECIPES

Many recipes are available
for preparing and cooking clams.
Here are a selected few...

CLAM CHOWDER

1 pound bacon, diced
1/2 pound ham, cubed
4 cups onion, chopped
1/4 cup flour
12 cups potatoes, diced

6 cups clams, undrained
  minced
7 cups milk
Salt and pepper to taste

Sauté the bacon and ham, drain off most of the bacon drippings and save. Add the onion to bacon and ham mixture; sauté until the onion is limp. Stir in the flour. Pour enough bacon drippings back into the pan to fry the potatoes. Add the potatoes and fry, stirring constantly, about 15 minutes or until the potatoes are soft. Add the clams with liquid and cook 5 more minutes. Add milk; season with salt and pepper to taste. Dot with butter or margarine when serving. **SERVES 12-16**

CLAM SAUCE FOR SPAGHETTI

1 pound spaghetti
3 tablespoons butter
2/3 cup light cream
1 cup sauteed minced clams

2-3 tablespoons Parmesan
  cheese
1/8 pound Cheddar
  cheese, grated

Cook spaghetti; drain and return to pan. Reheat slowly and add remaining ingredients, one at a time, mixing well after each addition. **SERVES 4-6**

CLAM DIP

1 8-ounce package creamed cheese
1 cup clams, minced and sauteed
1 tablespoon mayonnaise
1/4 teaspoon garlic salt
Crackers or chips

1 tablespoon
   Worcestershire sauce
1/4 teaspoon
   monosodium glutamate

Mix all ingredients in order listed. Use reserved clam juice to obtain the right consistency. Chill for 5-6 days before serving. Serve with crackers or chips.

BAKED CLAMS

1 pint cleaned clams
1/2 cup salad oil
1 teaspoon salt
1 tablespoon chopped onion

1/2 cup grated cheddar
   cheese
1 cup dry bread crumbs

Combine oil, salt and onion. Place clams in mixture for 1 minute. Remove and drain, then roll in cheese and then in bread crumbs. Place in a well-greased baking pan and bake in a hot oven at 450° for 12 minutes or until nicely browned. **SERVES 6**

MANHATTAN CLAM CHOWDER

1 pint clams and liquid
1/2 cup diced bacon
1 medium onion, chopped
1 cup diced raw potatoes
2 cups water

1 can (20 oz.) tomatoes
1 teaspoon salt
1/8 teaspoon pepper
1/8 teaspoon thyme
1/2 bay leaf

Sauté bacon in large sauce pan until crisp. Add onion and fry for about 5 minutes, or until tender. Add potato, bay leaf and water. Simmer for 10 to 15 minutes or until potatoes are done. Add the rest of the ingredients and heat until hot, but do not boil.

SERVES 6

CLAMBAKE

Dig a large hole. Line it with wet stones (taken from the water) and build a hot fire in the pit. Let the stones heat for 2 or 3 hours. Shovel out the hot coals and place a layer of wet seaweed in the pit. Cover it with chicken wire, then add another layer of seaweed. Put in the clams. Often potatoes and unhusked ears of corn are added to the pit. Cover again with seaweed and finally a tarpaulin. Weigh down the edges of the tarp with stones, then shovel a little sand over the top of the tarp. Allow to steam for approximately 2 hours. Halves of chicken and lobster are sometimes added to the clambake. Serve bowls or cups of hot clam chowder as the first course and watermelon for dessert.

CLAM PATTIES

1-1/4 cups minced clams
2 cups cooked, mashed potatoes
2 tablespoons butter or margarine
1/2 teaspoon salt

1/4 teaspoon pepper
1 tablespoon lemon juice
2 eggs slightly beaten

Drain minced clams and combine with mashed potatoes, butter, salt and lemon juice. Add beaten eggs; mix well. Shape into 12 patties of equal size and fry in hot fat until lightly browned on both sides.   **SERVES 6**

STIR-FRY STEAMERS

3 pounds cleaned steamer clams
1 cup chinese chives or cilantro
2 tablespoons white wine
1-1/2 tablespoons soy sauce
1 teaspoon corn starch
1/2 cup vegetable oil
5 hot red peppers (optional)
1 tablespoon ginger (chopped)

1 cup red pepper
  (chopped)
1/2 teaspoon sugar
1 teaspoon garlic
  (chopped)
1-1/2 tablespoons black
  beans (optional)
1/2 cup water

In a wok, heat oil until hot. Add ginger and garlic. Carefully spoon in clams, black beans, sugar and red bell peppers. Stir well. Prepare a mixture of the soy sauce, cornstarch and water; add to the clams. Pour in wine and red hot peppers. Stir clams well until all clams have opened. Serve in a large, low bowl; adding chives to the top of the clams.

SERVES 3-4

SPORT CRABBING IN CALIFORNIA

Two species of crabs in California waters,
the Dungeness (left) and the Red Rock Crab (right)

Crabbing along California's breathtaking Humboldt Bay or Tomales Bay is a totally unique outdoor experience that you simply must try to fully appreciate. Just imagine for a minute waking up early on a mild June morning, packing a picnic lunch for the whole family, and heading out for a day of crabbing. You launch your boat and head out into the bay, dumping 5 or 6 baited crab rings over the side as you go. After an anxious 20 minutes you set a course back for the bobbing floats and pull the rings up fast so the catch can't escape. The first pull reveals half a dozen scrambling dungeness crabs and two are keepers. Several smaller, but very tasty, red rock crabs are also part of the catch. Anxious and excited brothers and sisters compete to pull up each crab ring and soon there are enough crabs to head to the rocky shoreline and begin boiling the ocean-fresh salt water to cook the crabs. An hour later and a few more runs back to the rings and there are plenty of scrumptious crabs to feed the entire family with enough left over for a crab salad back at home.

By the time the day is over, all the family is ready for bed but anxious to return and do it all again. And why not? Fresh salt air, an inexpensive outdoor family adventure, and topped off with a meal of the finest seafood that California has to offer.

A variety of crab species inhabit California marine waters, but the dungeness crab is what California sport crabbing is all about. The dungeness is mostly a deep-sea ocean dweller, but north of Monterey Bay good numbers of these 1 to 3-pound crustaceans inhabit many bays and estuaries throughout the year. Once you travel south of Monterey Bay, dungeness crabs become increasingly scarce, but considerable numbers of several crabs collectively referred to as "rock crabs" are caught. These are the rock, red, slender and yellow crabs. Rock crabs have great flavor, but they have meat mainly in their large, distinguishing black claws. Dungeness cannot be harvested inside San Francisco Bay but the rock crabs are fair game.

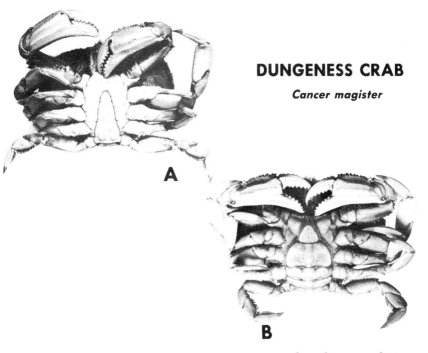

DUNGENESS CRAB

Cancer magister

A

B

Dungeness crab, *Cancer magister.* Underside view of (A) a male crab, 7 inches across the back, (B) a female crab, 6 inches across the back.

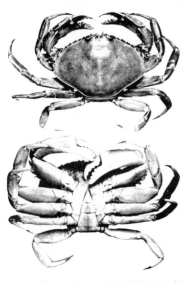

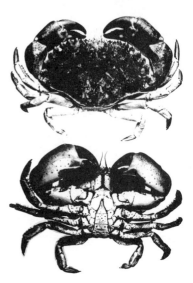

Slender crab, *Cancer gracilis*. Top and bottom views of a 2¼ inch male specimen.

Rock crab, *Cancer antennarius*. Top and bottom views of a male crab, 5 inches across the back.

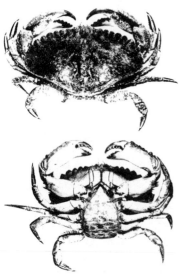

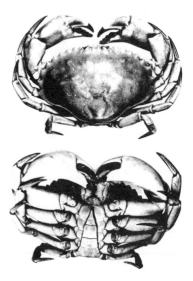

Red crab, *Cancer productus*. The upper photograph shows the top surface of a 6½ inch male. The lower photograph shows the under surface of a 5¾ inch female crab.

Yellow crab, *Cancer anthonyi*. Top and bottom views of a male crab, 6 inches across the back.

Photo courtesy of California Dept. of Fish and Game

California "Rock Crabs"

Dungeness crabs start life as a free-swimming larvae form, called a megalaps, which are consumed by practically every fish species in the sea. By the end of their first year of life they have grown and shed several shells, a process known as "molting." They shed their shells frequently during their second and third years of life and reach full body size and weight by their fourth year. They often live to be 10 years of age. They larger crabs most frequently "molt" in late summer and fall and their shells are often soft at this time. Soft-shelled crabs have poor flavor and low meat content and should be released upon capture. In California, only dungeness crabs 5-3/4 inches measured across the shell in front of the spines are legal. Check current regulations to see the correct size and limit for the area you are crabbing. The daily limit is 10 dungeness per person. All other California crabs have a limit per person of 35 and they must be at least 4 inches across the back at the widest part. Again, be sure to consult the most current regulations before going crabbing. Most local sporting goods stores have them.

Crabs are opportunistic feeders and will eat practically any clam, fish or other ocean organism they can find or catch. They prefer fresh food or bait.

A Red Rock Crab (left) compared to a Dungeness Crab.

EQUIPMENT

Crab rings are the most frequently used type of harvest equipment here in California. A small metal ring about a foot or so in diameter forms the bottom and a larger metal ring 24 to 30 inches across the top. They are joined by heavy fishing web or knotted mesh that covers the sides and bottom. A three-way rope is attached to the larger ring. A bright colored and highly visible float attached to the end of the rope helps the crabber locate his rings once they are "set." A 50-foot length of rope is about right for most situations. Bait is secured to the bottom mesh. When the ring is lowered into the water the large ring and mesh collapse onto the smaller ring and the whole affair lays flat on the bottom. When sufficient time has passed and hopefully crabs are feeding on the bait, the ring is swiftly pulled to the surface and the crabs are caught in the funnel-like trap.

The most common equipment used for crabbing in California are: (left to right) The Pot, Ring, and folding crab trap. (photo by Jason Campbell).

Crab rings are fairly inexpensive (they can be purchased for under $20 or can be rented for about $5 per day) and work fine, but they do have a couple of drawbacks. Some California marine waters have good numbers of extremely intelligent harbor seals and sea lions that have learned to steal a free meal, namely your crab bait, from the open and unprotected crab rings. Traps and pots that protect the bait inside eliminate this problem. Another problem with rings is that crabs feeding on bait inside the ring are free to come and go. Frequent ring checks are necessary. Also, a swift and steady pull is required to keep crabs from escaping upon retrieval.

Crab pots are deadly crab catchers. They are simply two large metal rings separated a foot or so by bars and covered with wire mesh. They have one or two one-way entrances just large enough to allow crabs to enter but not escape. The advantages of crab pots over crab rings are that seals cannot steal your bait, entering crabs cannot easily escape, and frequent checks are unnecessary. Disadvantages are that they are heavy, quite bulky and fairly expensive (about $70). Lose one of these and you will cry! Again, a 50-foot length of rope and float is necessary.

The folding crab trap is effective and folds up for easy storage. Mark Vargas demonstrates use of the folding trap.

The collapsible square metal trap is one of the most ingenious inventions to come along in years. They keep seals out, catch and hold crabs well, are less expensive and more available than pots, and they fold up for easy storage. In my opinion, these traps are the only way to go.

Several types of crab snares are on the market and they work fairly well using a stiff fishing pole with heavy line. Specialized garden rakes can be used to rake for crabs in "crab holes" left by the receding tide along the open beach line. These same rakes with long handles can be used to retrieve crabs spotted in the clear, shallow waters of some bays and estuaries. A rake modified into a scoop attached to a long handle can also be used to retrieve crabs. Rakes used for crabbing should have the tines covered to prevent damage to undersized crabs.

California law requires that every person taking species having a size limit must have a measuring device. Measurers can be made or purchased from most sport shops near crabbing areas and are much more convenient than a ruler or metal tape. Again, only dungeness crabs measuring 5-3/4 inches across the back are legal for sport harvest in California.

A large 5-gallon kettle is a good idea if you intend to cook crabs yourself either on the beach or at home.

Good foul weather clothes and rubber knee boots are more than a good idea even in California. Waders are needed for crabbing from shore. No matter if you crab from a boat, dock or pier, hope for sunny skies, but be prepared for cooler, wet weather. It's fine if you don't need them, but not having the proper gear can turn a great adventure into a nightmare.

Kai Johnson with a nice Crab caught while crabbing from a dock.

HOW, WHEN AND WHERE TO CRAB

The bait you use to lure crabs into your ring, pot or trap can fill your boat with plenty of scrambling crabs or send you scrambling to the nearest seafood market to pay an arm and a leg for a few not-so-fresh crab. Any fresh or frozen meat will attract crabs, but some are better than others. Fish carcasses of any kind make excellent bait and a few sport shops carry frozen shad which I consider the ultimate crab bait. Fresh or frozen clams placed in bait containers also work very well. Good crab bait can be purchased from many outlets along the coast and bays. Remember, however, nothing is worse than running out of bait when these "sea-spiders" are really thick. Bait size and type are an individual choice, but be sure to secure it with wire or twine in the trap because currents or crabs will carry it away.

Many northern California bays and estuaries have good populations of dungeness and rock crabs. Most notable are Humboldt, Bodega, Tomales and Half Moon bays, and Elkhorn Slough. Traps and pots are set with the use of boats and from harbor docks and piers. The amount of fresh water entering these huge estuaries from the rivers that feed them will determine just how good the crabbing will be. Summer and fall months have the least rainfall and are the best time to crab. September and October are often the premium months for crab harvest.

All coastal bays are affected by the tides and so are the feeding habits of crabs. These critters are most active and easiest to catch when the tide is nearest to high or low slack. When the tidal current runs hard, either going in or out, this is when crabs bury themselves, don't feed, and wait for the water to slow down. Usually the best time to crab is 1 hour before and after low or high tide. Crabbing is also best when there is little difference between high and

Crabbing off the docks can be fun and productive.

Crabbing from a boat.

low tide as this is when tidal currents are less severe. For example, try to pick a day where there is a *high* low tide and a *low* high tide. Under ideal conditions, this sport can be relatively good the entire 12-hour tide.

In coastal bays or estuaries where seasonal and daily fresh water fluctuations occur, harvest areas are more specific. In general, the lower in the bay and the closer to the ocean, the better the crabbing will be.

The Crab ring is probably the most common method
for sport crab harvest in California.
photo courtesy of Washington Dept. of Fisheries

COOKING AND CLEANING

The most accepted method for cooking crabs is to boil them in salt water. Pure ocean water has a salt content of 35 parts per thousand and this is ideal to cook crabs. If you are cooking your crabs at coastal estuaries, use water taken at near high tide and close to the mouth. Water used on the outgoing tide or from the upper reaches of the bay will generally not have the desired salt content. When you cook crabs at home, add enough salt to the water to simulate the taste of ocean water.

Drop the crabs into the water once it has come to a full boil. Boil the crabs for a full 20 minutes, pull them from the water, and allow them to cool before cleaning.

The cleaning of crabs is really easy. Simply pull the back shell away from the body and legs and then remove the feather-like gills and the yellow or orange organs. Most of the organs can easily be taken out with your fingers and the rest can be washed out with water.

Removing crabmeat from the shell is a messy business at best. I spread a thick layer of newspaper over the entire table and have at it. Only experience will determine the best way to get at the scrumptious meat, but nutcrackers and a pointed utensil are very helpful. The flavor of fresh-caught crabmeat is undescribably delicious and definitely well worth the effort.

The meat of a crab is extremely perishable whether cooked or not, and it should be kept on ice if at all possible. Crabmeat should be eaten within 24 hours if you do not intend to freeze it.

REGULATIONS

CRAB

- See California Sport Fishing Regulations for complete and current information on catch limits, equipment and closures.
- Fishing hours are one-half hour before sunrise to one-half hour after sunset.
- Crabs may be brought to the surface for measuring, but all undersized crabs must immediately be returned to the water.

Species	Area	Season	Size Limit	Daily Limit
Dungeness	Del Norte, Humboldt, Mendocino counties	Dec 1 - Jul 30	5-3/4"	10
	All other counties	2nd Tuesday in November thru Jul 30	5-3/4"	10
Yellow, Rock, Red and slender crab species	Pacific Ocean bays and estuaries	All year	4"	35

Crabbing is great family-oriented fun!

Kids seem to enjoy crabbing as much as adults.

RECIPES

Many recipes are available
for preparing and cooking crabs.
Here are a selected few...

CRAB FRITTERS

1/2 pound crabmeat
2-1/2 tablespoons chopped onion
1 tablespoon chopped parsley
1 tablespoon chopped green pepper
2 tablespoons chopped ripe tomato
2 eggs
1 teaspoon Worcestershire sauce

1/4 cup flour
2 teaspoons baking
  powder
1/8 teaspoon salt
3 tablespoons butter
Lemon wedges

Thoroughly mix together the first seven ingredients. Sift the flour, baking powder and salt into the first mixture. Stir until just blended. Fry by tablespoonfuls in hot butter over moderate-high heat, turning once to brown on both sides. Serve immediately accompanied by lemon wedges. **SERVES 4-6**

CRAB CASSEROLE FOR FOUR

1 14-ounce can artichoke hearts,
  drained
1 4-ounce can sliced mushrooms,
  drained
1 pound fresh or frozen crabmeat,
  drained
2 tablespoons butter
2-1/2 tablespoons flour
Paprika

1/2 teaspoon salt
Dash cayenne pepper
1 cup half and half
2 tablespoon cereal
  crumbs
1 tablespoon grated
  parmesan cheese
2 tablespoon sherry

Cut artichoke hearts in half and place in well-greased, shallow 1-1/2 quart casserole. Cover with mushrooms and crabmeat. Melt butter and blend in flour and seasonings. Add cream gradually and cook until thick, stirring constantly. Stir in sherry. Pour sauce over crabmeat. Combine crumbs and cheese; sprinkle over sauce. Sprinkle with paprika. Bake in hot 450° oven for 12-15 minutes until bubbly. **SERVES 4**

ROLLS OF CRAB

1 pound American cheese, grated
2-1/2 green peppers, chopped
1/2 pint stuffed olives, chopped
1 cup butter, melted

3/4 pound crabmeat
1 cup tomato hot sauce
48 rolls (poppy seed,
    hard or potato)

Combine ingredients and fill scooped-out rolls. Wrap individually
in foil, twisting end. Let stand in refrigerator overnight. When
ready to use, put into covered pan and heat 1/2 hour at 350°.

BROILED CRAB SANDWICHES

1 6-ounce package cream cheese,
    softened
2 teaspoons lemon juice
1 cup flaked crabmeat
1 tablespoon onion, chopped

3/4 teaspoon chili
    powder to taste
1/8 teaspoon salt
2 tablespoons mayonnaise
4 english muffins, split

Mix first seven ingredients. Spread over english muffins and broil
until browned.

FETTUCCINE WITH CRAB

4 tablespoons butter
2 garlic cloves, minced
4 tablespoons flour
1/2 cup sherry or dry white wine
2 cups half and half
Cooked fettuccine

1/2 pound mushrooms,
    sliced
1/3 cup parmesan cheese
Salt and pepper
1-1/4 pound crabmeat

Melt 4 tablespoons butter in large skillet, add garlic and sauté
until soft. Add flour and cook briefly. Gradually add sherry and
half and half. Cook until sauce is smooth and thick; set aside.
Sauté mushrooms in generous amount of butter. Add mushrooms
and any juice to cream sauce. Stir in parmesan cheese and add
salt and pepper to taste. Gently fold in crabmeat. Heat through.
Serve over freshly cooked fettuccine, your own or store bought.

SERVES 6

SOUFFLÉ OF CRAB

10 slices bread, crust trimmed
3 cups crabmeat, tuna or shrimp
3/4 cup celery, chopped
3/4 cup onion, chopped
1/2 cup mayonnaise
1 cup green pepper, chopped
4 eggs
Paprika

3 cups milk
1/2 teaspoon salt
1 10-1/2 ounce can
  cream of mushroom
  soup, undiluted
Cheddar cheese, mild or
  sharp, grated

Butter a 9x13 inch baking dish and line with half of bread slices. Mix together next 5 ingredients and put on top of bread slices in baking dishes. Top with remainder of bread slices. Beat together the eggs, milk and salt. Pour egg mixture over bread and refrigerate overnight. Next day bake at 325° for 15 minutes. Remove from oven and spread undiluted soup over the top. Sprinkle with cheese and paprika. Return to oven and bake 1 hour longer. Allow to set 10-15 minutes before cutting.

SERVES 6-8

CRAB AND ARTICHOKE ELEGANTE

1/4 pound butter
3 tablespoons onion, minced
1/2 cup flour
1 quart cream, heated to the
  boiling point
1/2 cup madeira
Salt and pepper
2 tablespoons lemon juice
4 cups fresh crabmeat
Paprika

3 9-ounce packages
  frozen artichoke hearts,
  cooked according to
  directions or equal
  amount canned
  artichoke hearts
6 ounces spaghetti or
  linguini, cooked and
  drained
2 cups grated Gruyere or
  Swiss cheese, divided

Preheat oven to 350°. Melt butter in large heavy pan. When butter sizzles, add onion and sauté until golden. Stir in flour, cooking over low heat until flour is pale. Remove from heat. Add cream, stirring vigorously. Return to moderate heat and stir until sauce reaches a boil. Reduce heat and add Madeira. Season with salt and pepper; set aside. Pour lemon juice over crabmeat and toss lightly. Quarter artichoke hearts. Combine crab and artichoke hearts. Add cream sauce. Toss crab mixture with pasta and place in a 6-quart buttered casserole dish. Stir in half of grated cheese. Sprinkle remaining cheese on top and dust with paprika. Bake 25-30 minutes or until heated through. **SERVES 10-12**

Crabbing from small boats is fun and quite effective.

A long sport crabber retrieves his crab ring from a pier in the fog.

GENERAL

POLLUTION

Pollution of shellfish beds is a growing problem in California's marine waters. As a result, clams and other bivalve shellfish may be contaminated with bacteria, viruses or chemicals. To protect public health, some sport and commercial shellfish beds have been closed to harvest. San Francisco Bay is now contaminated and several other areas are threatened. Before taking clams or mussels, be sure they are safe to eat by contacting the California Department of Public Health. Their telephone number is (510) 540-3423. They follow the condition of bivalves carefully throughout the year. Do not harvest shellfish from areas posted as contaminated.

RED TIDE (Paralytic Shellfish Poisoning)

Paralytic Shellfish Poisoning (PSP) occurs when clams, oysters, scallops and mussels consume and concentrate a microscopic algae which contains a powerful toxin. The color of the water is no indication that the shellfish are safe to eat. Many harmless algae may color the water red, while rarely is the water red where PSP occurs. In addition, cooking does not reduce the extreme toxicity. High concentrations of this toxin can result in sickness and, in some cases, death. To be sure the shellfish are safe to eat, contact the California Department of Public Health. NOTE: Harvesting of certain shellfish is closed from May 1 to October 31 because of the risk of PSP. Be sure to check with the California Department of Public Health to be on the safe side. Their telephone number is (510) 540-3423.

DOMOIC ACID

Domoic acid is a naturally occurring toxin that may accumulate in filter-feeding fish and shellfish. Cooking does not destroy this toxin. Occurring in North America, first in Canada in 1987, cases of poisoning involving razor clams in southern Washington were reported in 1991. This led California to advise consumers not to eat razor clams and mussels for a short period of time. Call the California Department of Health if you have any questions or concerns.

SAFETY TIPS

During any mussel quarantine period, thoroughly clean and wash all bivalve shellfish before cooking and eating. Remove and discard the viscera of all clams. To be safe, contact the County Department of Environmental Health for the area you are planning to visit. Telephone numbers are provided.

Let's not let this happen to our splendid natural resources.

APPENDIX A

CALIFORNIA COUNTY DEPARTMENTS OF ENVIRONMENTAL HEALTH

COASTAL COUNTIES

Del Norte - (707) 464-7227

Humboldt - (707) 445-6215

Los Angeles - (213) 881-4000

Marin - (415) 554-2720

Mendocino - (707) 464-4466

Monterey - (415) 755-4540

Orange - (714) 667-3771

San Diego - (619) 338-2222

San Francisco - (415) 554-2720

San Luis Obispo - (805) 549-5544

San Mateo - (415) 363-4305

Santa Barbara - (805) 681-5200

Santa Cruz - (408) 425-2341

Sonoma - (707) 525-6500

Ventura - (805) 654-2818

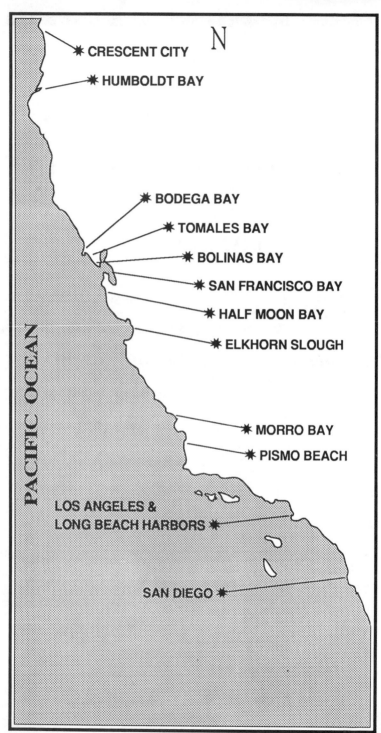

N

* CRESCENT CITY

* HUMBOLDT BAY

PACIFIC OCEAN

* BODEGA BAY

* TOMALES BAY

* BOLINAS BAY

* SAN FRANCISCO BAY

* HALF MOON BAY

* ELKHORN SLOUGH

* MORRO BAY

* PISMO BEACH

LOS ANGELES &
LONG BEACH HARBORS *

SAN DIEGO *

CALIFORNIA BAYS

California bays, also called estuaries, are a unique environment where fresh and salt water meet forming a fish and wildlife habitat type found nowhere else on earth. Since time began man has been attracted to these coastal bays for both recreation and food gathering. Today we are no different in that we still like to go to the bays for food and fun.

We are very fortunate here in California to have a large number of estuaries both large and small to fulfill our recreational needs. I have provided maps of the major estuaries here in California where significant numbers of clams and crabs are available for public recreational harvest. I have tried to accurately describe where clams and crabs are found and locations of some public access areas. I've also provided tips on how to find and harvest them. This is not to say that you won't find good clamming and crabbing in other California waters that I didn't have room to cover in this book. I also encourage you to ask questions at local tackle shops and sporting goods stores or just ask people. Clam diggers and crabbers are usually some of the friendliest people you'll meet, and my experience is they'll be happy to share information with you. I hope this will help in selecting a site and planning your next coastal clam digging or crabbing experience.

After that last clam is dug or crab caught, take a little time to look around at the wildlife and scenery that surround you, and think about the wonderful time you have enjoyed. Estuaries are extremely sensitive and vulnerable to man's activities. These California bays are Mother Nature's gift to all of us now and for our children in the future. Enjoy them and preserve them.

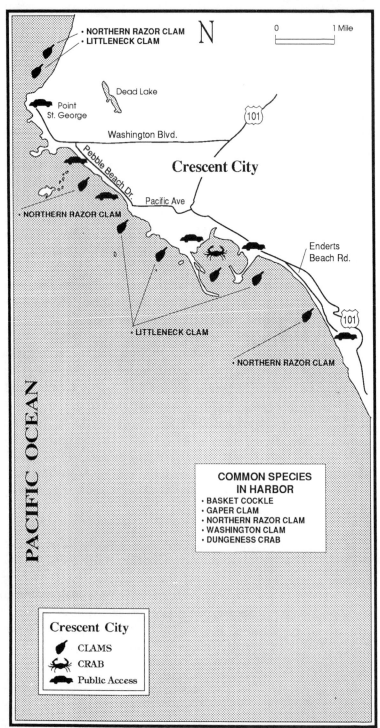

N

0   1 Mile

- NORTHERN RAZOR CLAM
- LITTLENECK CLAM

Dead Lake

Point
St. George

Washington Blvd.

101

Crescent City

Pebble Beach Dr.

Pacific Ave

• NORTHERN RAZOR CLAM

Enderts
Beach Rd.

• LITTLENECK CLAM

101

• NORTHERN RAZOR CLAM

PACIFIC OCEAN

**COMMON SPECIES
IN HARBOR**
- BASKET COCKLE
- GAPER CLAM
- NORTHERN RAZOR CLAM
- WASHINGTON CLAM
- DUNGENESS CRAB

Crescent City

CLAMS

CRAB

Public Access

CRESCENT CITY

This bay, located off Hwy 101 79 miles north of Eureka and 22 miles south of the Oregon border, offers a good opportunity for sport harvesting of razor, littleneck, cockle, gaper and Washington clams as well as dungeness crabs.

Pebble Beach Public Fishing Access at the end of Pacific Avenue has littleneck clams. You'll find additional access along Pebble Beach Drive between Point St. George and Battery Point. Also, try Enderts Beach, three miles south of Crescent City, for razor clams, and you should find softshells in the mudflats in Lake Talawa. Several public piers, tackle shops, boat rentals, fuel and boat launching can be found at the Small Boat Basin, Citizen's Dock and Bayshore Marinas. Several motels are also available near the bay.

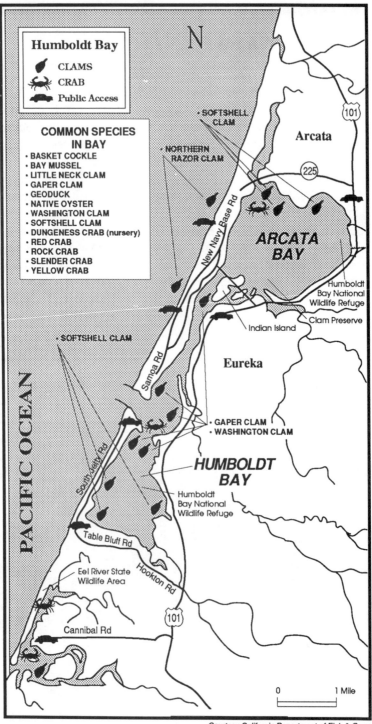

Humboldt Bay

- CLAMS
- CRAB
- Public Access

COMMON SPECIES IN BAY
- BASKET COCKLE
- BAY MUSSEL
- LITTLE NECK CLAM
- GAPER CLAM
- GEODUCK
- NATIVE OYSTER
- WASHINGTON CLAM
- SOFTSHELL CLAM
- DUNGENESS CRAB (nursery)
- RED CRAB
- ROCK CRAB
- SLENDER CRAB
- YELLOW CRAB

N

• SOFTSHELL CLAM

Arcata

101

225

• NORTHERN RAZOR CLAM

New Navy Base Rd

ARCATA BAY

Humboldt Bay National Wildlife Refuge

Clam Preserve

Indian Island

Eureka

Samoa Rd

• SOFTSHELL CLAM

PACIFIC OCEAN

• GAPER CLAM
• WASHINGTON CLAM

HUMBOLDT BAY

South Jetty Rd

Humboldt Bay National Wildlife Refuge

Table Bluff Rd

Hookton Rd

Eel River State Wildlife Area

101

Cannibal Rd

0   1 Mile

Courtesy California Department of Fish & Game

HUMBOLDT BAY

This large bay, including Arcata Bay at its northern end, offers some of the very best opportunities for California sport clamming and crabbing. It is located on Hwy 101 at the city of Eureka.

Opportunity to harvest red and rock crabs abound in the bays. Dungeness crab can be taken nearer to the mouth. Cockles, mussels, gapers, littlenecks, geoducks, Washingtons and softshells are all common to both of these bays, but access is best in the central and southern areas. Razor clamming is popular on the sandy, clean ocean beaches around Eureka. This bay is unique in California in that there are populations of native oysters in this bay and, if located, can be harvested by sport diggers. About 45 percent of California's commercial oyster production takes place in the northern bay. These commercial areas are well marked, so please don't intrude. Several good areas to try for native oysters are around King Salmon and the mouth of the Mad River. To the south, at Crab County Park in the Eel River delta, you can enjoy softshell clamming and dungeness crabbing.

Numerous bait and tackle stores, boat ramps and facilities are available to make your visit an enjoyable one. In addition to the great clamming and crabbing, the area offers excellent access to bay and ocean areas, and a wide assortment of accommodations and attractions for visitors.

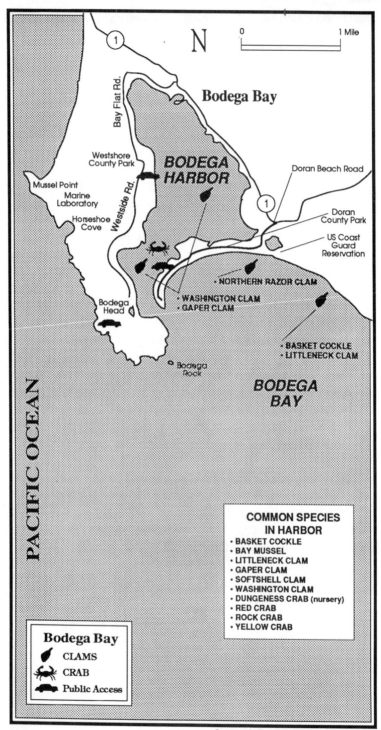

N

0   1 Mile

Bodega Bay

Bay Flat Rd.

BODEGA HARBOR

Westshore County Park

Doran Beach Road

Mussel Point Marine Laboratory

Westside Rd.

Horseshoe Cove

Doran County Park

US Coast Guard Reservation

• NORTHERN RAZOR CLAM

• WASHINGTON CLAM
• GAPER CLAM

Bodega Head

• BASKET COCKLE
• LITTLENECK CLAM

Bodega Rock

BODEGA BAY

PACIFIC OCEAN

COMMON SPECIES IN HARBOR
• BASKET COCKLE
• BAY MUSSEL
• LITTLENECK CLAM
• GAPER CLAM
• SOFTSHELL CLAM
• WASHINGTON CLAM
• DUNGENESS CRAB (nursery)
• RED CRAB
• ROCK CRAB
• YELLOW CRAB

Bodega Bay
CLAMS
CRAB
Public Access

Courtesy California Department of Fish & Game

94

BODEGA BAY

Bodega Bay is located about 50 miles north of San Francisco just off Hwy 1. It is a beautiful town and happens to be one of Northern California's busiest fishing ports. At low tide, this shallow 800 acre bay offers up gaper and Washington clams as well as red, rock and an occasional dungeness crab. Mason's Marina on Westside Road, Spud Point Marina and Doran Regional Park offer launching facilities and access to clamming areas.

Everyone enjoys a good day of crabbing at Bodega Bay.

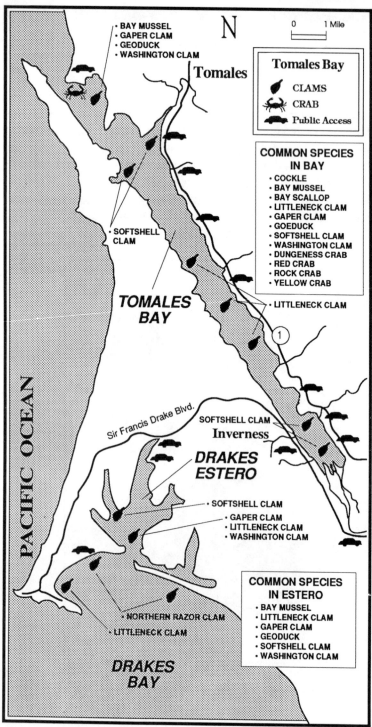

Courtesy California Department of Fish & Game

96

TOMALES BAY

This large bay is 13 miles long, one mile wide and very shallow throughout. It is not a true estuary in the sense that very little fresh water mixes with the salty ocean water. It does, however, offer excellent littleneck clamming. Other clams found here are gaper, Washington, geoduck and softshell. Dungeness and rock crabs are also present in Tomales Bay and available to the sportsman. Several commercial oyster companies do business along the bay and sell some of the finest and <u>freshest</u> oysters you'll find anywhere on the West Coast. Some of the best clamming takes place at Heart's Desire and Pebble Beach in Tomales Bay State Park and near Marshall and Hog Island on the east side of the bay. NOTE: A "Clammer's Ferry" takes diggers from Lawson's Landing, near Sand Point, to the mudflats around Hog Island at low tides to dig for Washington and horseneck clams.

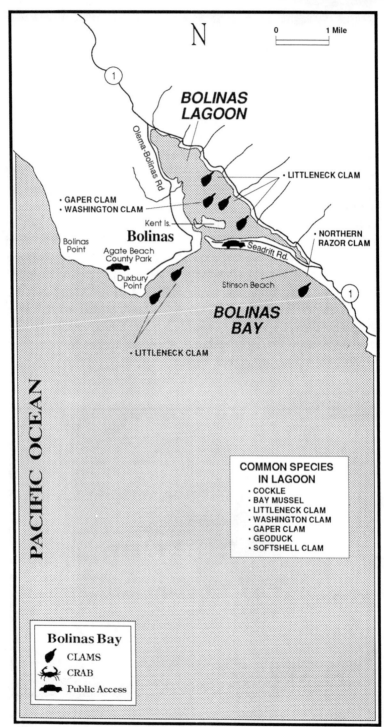

N

0   1 Mile

BOLINAS
LAGOON

Olema-Bolinas Rd.

• LITTLENECK CLAM

• GAPER CLAM
• WASHINGTON CLAM

Kent Is.

Bolinas

Bolinas
Point

Agate Beach
County Park

Duxbury
Point

Seadrift Rd.

• NORTHERN
RAZOR CLAM

Stinson Beach

1

BOLINAS
BAY

• LITTLENECK CLAM

PACIFIC OCEAN

**COMMON SPECIES
IN LAGOON**
• COCKLE
• BAY MUSSEL
• LITTLENECK CLAM
• WASHINGTON CLAM
• GAPER CLAM
• GEODUCK
• SOFTSHELL CLAM

Bolinas Bay

CLAMS
CRAB
Public Access

Courtesy California Department of Fish & Game

98

BOLINAS LAGOON

The town of Bolinas, on the west side of Bolinas Lagoon, is a small, quiet residential community and difficult to find. It is just off of Hwy 1 about 20 miles north of San Francisco. When you reach the north end of the lagoon, take the unmarked left turn and circle back around about a mile or two to town. There are few facilities in town, but they have some nice restaurants and shops.

The lagoon itself offers good access along the east shore and is home to a variety of clams. The most common are littleneck, gaper and Washington. The sandy spit protecting the lagoon from the southwest has some numbers of razor clams. Duxbury Reef is a marine reserve and permission from the Department of Fish and Game is required to remove any marine species.

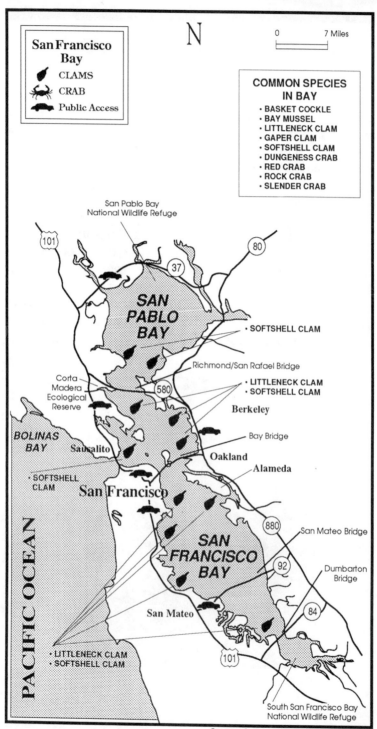

Courtesy California Department of Fish & Game

SAN FRANCISCO BAY

San Francisco Bay and its waterways contain 90 percent of California's remaining coastal wetlands and are among the best areas for clamming and crabbing anywhere in California. However, due to suspected pollution levels, it has been closed for a number of years. I've included this map with the hope that someday we will succeed in restoring this magnificent natural wonder to its pristine state and that it will once again be opened for clamming.

San Francisco Bay is closed to sport dungeness crab harvesting.

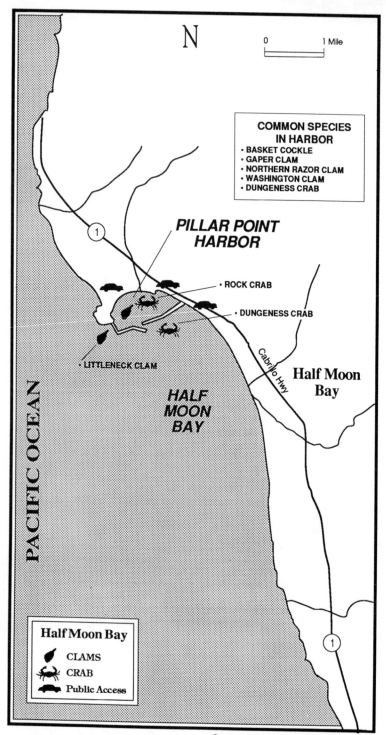

N

0   1 Mile

**COMMON SPECIES
IN HARBOR**
- BASKET COCKLE
- GAPER CLAM
- NORTHERN RAZOR CLAM
- WASHINGTON CLAM
- DUNGENESS CRAB

*PILLAR POINT
HARBOR*

• ROCK CRAB

• DUNGENESS CRAB

Cabrillo Hwy

**Half Moon
Bay**

• LITTLENECK CLAM

*HALF
MOON
BAY*

PACIFIC OCEAN

Half Moon Bay

CLAMS

CRAB

Public Access

Courtesy California Department of Fish & Game

HALF MOON BAY

This beautiful bay is well within easy reach of San Francisco and lies along the scenic stretch of Hwy 1 between San Francisco and Santa Cruz. It can also be reached from Hwy 92 and is about 20 miles west of San Francisco Bay. Actually Pillar Point Harbor on the north end of the bay is where you will find the best clamming and crabbing. Good access can be found at Johnson's Pier, and there is a fishing pier near the Port Authority office that offers good rock crabbing.

Cockles, gapers, geoducks, littlenecks and Washingtons can be found in varying numbers in the mudflats of this gorgeous harbor.

The marina is very modern and clean. It offers boat ramps, clean restrooms, ample parking, charter boats and several wonderful seafood restaurants with some spectacular sunset views.

Also of note is a sport crabbing opportunity at the L-shaped Pacifica Municipal Pier, 15 miles north of Half Moon Bay. It's open 24 hours a day, and there is a bait and tackle shop where you can buy crab rings, bait and fishing supplies.

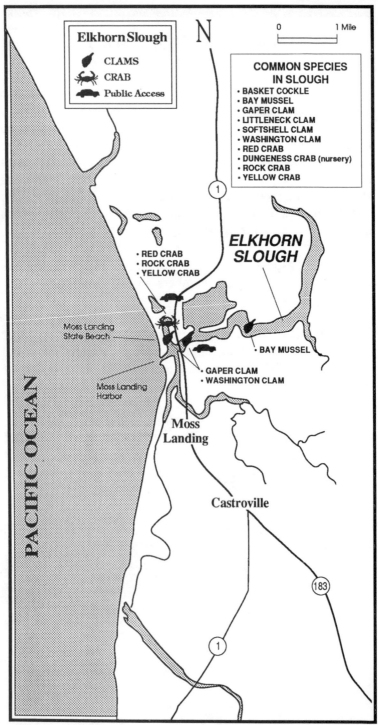

Courtesy California Department of Fish & Game

ELKHORN SLOUGH

This small seasonal estuary includes Moss Landing Harbor and is crossed by Hwy 1 about 15 miles north of Monterey and 30 miles south of Santa Cruz. It offers sport clamming and rock crabbing. The north harbor is popular for littleneck, gaper and Washington clams. These plus bay mussels, cockles, and softshells can be found throughout the slough. You'll find rock and yellow crabs in this bay.

Facilities available include a boat ramp, restrooms and parking. Moss Landing also has a sport fishing fleet, several good seafood restuarants and fish markets nearby. Moss Landing is also home to a number of small, exquisite antique shops for those who may not want to dig clams all day.

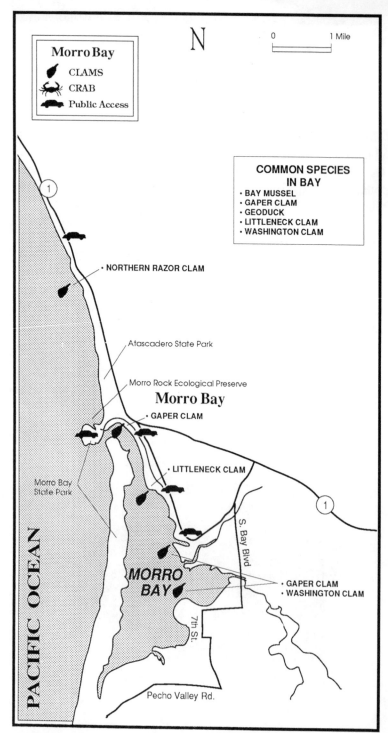

Courtesy California Department of Fish & Game

MORRO BAY

This scenic bay, named for the large conical rock near its mouth, is 15 miles northwest of San Luis Obispo just off Hwy 1. It offers good sport harvesting of clams and crab. Washington and geoduck clams are most common, but there are smaller populations of gapers, littlenecks, cockles and bay mussels in the intertidal mudflats throughout the bay. The sandy beaches north of the bay contain pockets of razor clams.

There are four public piers around Morro Bay and can be used for sport fishing and crabbing. From the Morro Bay Marina you can ride the "Clam Taxi" to the sand spit. From the south "T" pier you can rent boats for ocean fishing. The north "T" pier is a popular place for sport crabbing enthusiasts.

Morro Bay is oriented to tourists and provides excellent accommodations. It is also one of the more important commercial fishing centers in California.

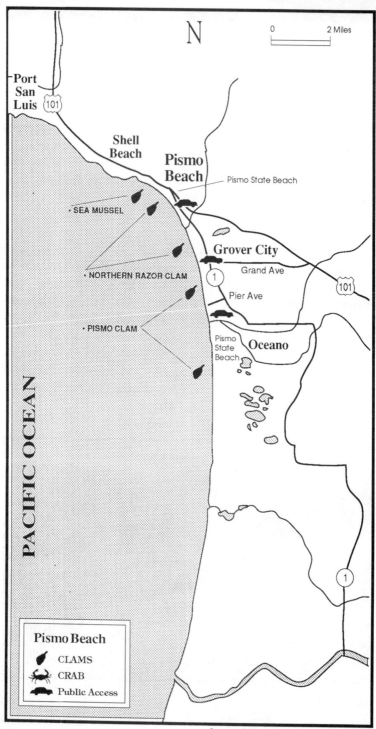

N

0   2 Miles

Port
San
Luis — (101)

Shell
Beach

Pismo
Beach — Pismo State Beach

• SEA MUSSEL

Grover City

Grand Ave

(1)

• NORTHERN RAZOR CLAM

Pier Ave

• PISMO CLAM

Oceano

Pismo
State
Beach

(101)

(1)

PACIFIC OCEAN

(1)

Pismo Beach

🦪 CLAMS

🦀 CRAB

🚗 Public Access

Courtesy California Department of Fish & Game

108

PISMO BEACH

Pismo Beach lies on a scenic stretch of US 101 near San Luis Obispo, 10 miles to the north. Although it is not an estuary, Pismo Beach offers a unique opportunity to the sport clamming enthusiast.

Here, the Pismo clam is found in large numbers. Access to the clamming beaches is excellent because you can drive onto the beach in the areas near Grover city and Oceano. It is also possible to find razor clams along parts of these beaches. Be sure to check current regulations or check at the Park Service gate at the beach access for locations of Pismo clam preserve areas. Sport rock crabbers should also try Port San Luis, 10 miles north of Pismo Beach. Facilities include piers, sport shops and charter boats.

Pismo Beach is a beautiful seaside resort area with excellent accommodations and attractions for visitors from the San Joaquin Valley and coastal "migrants."

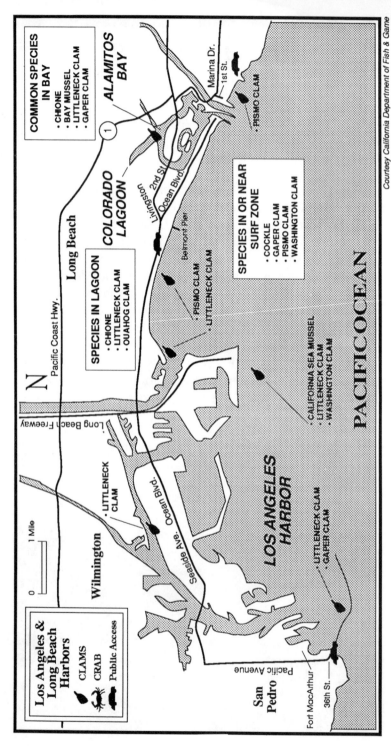

Courtesy California Department of Fish & Game

LOS ANGELES
and
LONG BEACH HARBORS

This large harbor facility has become the largest artificial harbor complex in the world. It includes Los Angeles and Long Beach Harbors. Alamitos Bay, Seal Beach and Colorado Lagoon are also very close by.

The most common clam here is the littleneck, although Washington, chione and gaper clams are also common throughout the complex. Access is very restricted in many parts of the harbor, but there are a few areas for the sport clammers to try; probably the best opportunity is along the Cabrillo Beach area. You can enter this area through a park gate located off Pacific Avenue near 36th Street. Several sandy beach areas along the north bay shore, both sides of the breakwater and surf side provide opportunities to harvest clams. Also, try for pismo clams along the sandy beaches around the complex. The breakwater and pier offer some outstanding fishing so, if the clams aren't showing, take the fishing pole along. It's also a popular place to have a family picnic. Alamitos Bay also offers clamming for chiones, littlenecks, gapers and cockles. Try along the peninsula side of Naples Island and also along the surf for pismo clams. Seal Beach from the San Gabriel River to the pier is also known to kick up some occasional gapers, Washingtons and pismos. Colorado Lagoon has small populations of chiones, littlenecks and the rare quahog, or cherrystone, clam. Access here is pretty easy as it is surrounded by streets. Be sure to carefully clean any clams you take from these areas, especially the dark colored intestines. Watch out also for sunbathers on those nice Southern California days.

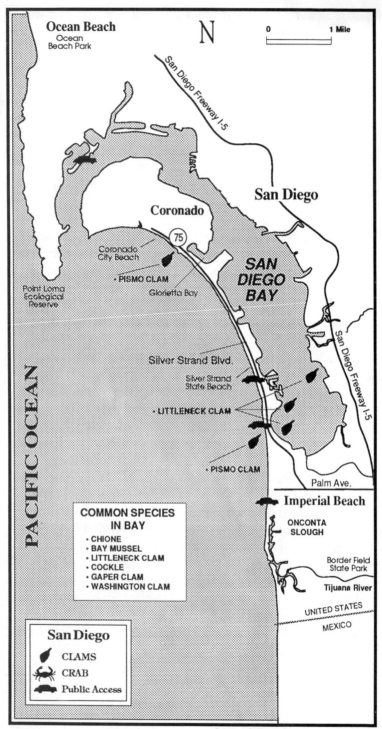

Ocean Beach
Ocean
Beach Park

N

0   1 Mile

San Diego Freeway I-5

San Diego

Coronado

(75)

Coronado
City Beach

· PISMO CLAM

Glorietta Bay

Point Loma
Ecological
Reserve

SAN DIEGO BAY

San Diego Freeway I-5

Silver Strand Blvd.

Silver Strand
State Beach

· LITTLENECK CLAM

PACIFIC OCEAN

· PISMO CLAM

Palm Ave.

Imperial Beach

ONCONTA
SLOUGH

Border Field
State Park

Tijuana River

UNITED STATES

MEXICO

COMMON SPECIES IN BAY
- CHIONE
- BAY MUSSEL
- LITTLENECK CLAM
- COCKLE
- GAPER CLAM
- WASHINGTON CLAM

San Diego

🦪 CLAMS

🦀 CRAB

🚗 Public Access

Courtesy California Department of Fish & Game

SAN DIEGO BAY

San Diego is the second largest city in California. It is modern, metropolitan and a year-round resort area. This large, natural bay offers a large variety of clams to the sportsperson, but access is rather limited. Inside the bay are littlenecks, chiones, cockles, gapers and Washington clams. Also, pismo clams can be found along the sandy, ocean beaches south of Silver Strand State Beach and near Coronado City Beach. Try some of the beaches on the bay-shore side of Silver Strand State Beach also. They may hold some concentrations of clams and are worth a look. Sweetwater Paradise Marsh Complex also has good concentrations of clams and is an excellent place to try.

Accommodations and attractions for visitors to the San Diego area will meet the needs of the most discerning.

Rock crabbing is family fun at Pillar Point Harbor in Half Moon Bay.

Docks can be an excellent place to crab.

Kai Johnson

Pillar Point Harbor

CONVENIENT ORDER FORM

YES! I want to order more copies of this book at $10.95 (include $1.00 postage per book). Discount 10% if ordering two to five books. Discount 20% if ordering six or more books. Please allow two weeks for delivery. Thanks.

NAME _____

ADDRESS _____

CITY _____ STATE _____ ZIP _____

Number of books being ordered _____

TOTAL AMOUNT ENCLOSED
(Check or Money Order) $_____

Mail to: **Adventure North Publishing Co.**
                  P.O. Box 1601
                  Waldport, Oregon 97394

Adventure North Publishing also publishes *"Clam Digging and Crabbing in Oregon," "Clam Digging and Crabbing in Washington," and "Oregon Hunting Guide."* For more information, write to the publisher at the above address.